1 MONTH OF
FREE
READING

at
www.ForgottenBooks.com

By purchasing this book you are eligible for one month membership to ForgottenBooks.com, giving you unlimited access to our entire collection of over 1,000,000 titles via our web site and mobile apps.

To claim your free month visit:
www.forgottenbooks.com/free1115809

ISBN 978-0-331-38448-2
PIBN 11115809

The Faculty

Mrs. Janie Sullivan
Education

Betty Short
Physical Education

Mrs. Stella Newsome
Literature

Ethel Burton
Librarian

Frank Cross, Chemistry

C. W. Paskins
Social Studies

Virginia Clements
Social Studies

J. W. Bedwell
Commerce

Robert James
Science

John H. Banks
Mathematics

Mrs. Carrie Lee Madden
Music

James Grisham
Bible

Mrs. A. M. Blount
Dietitian

W. A. Hogan
Bible

Andy Miller
Engineer

W. D. Shannon
Auto Mechanics

Faculty Homes

The 1946 WO-HE-LO

EDITORIAL STAFF

Editor. . . . . .Illene Richie
Sophomore Assistant. . . . . .Dixie Briggs
Freshman Assistant. . . . . Lynn Phillips
Literary Editor. . . . . .Mildred Lovorn
Assistant. . . . . .Ruth Mason
Feature Editor. . . . . Alene Martin
Assistant. . . . . Bonnie Hudson
Art Editor. . . . . Katherine Kemp
Assistant. . . . . .Joe Bennett
Organizations Editor. . . . . Katherine Cox
Assistant. . . . . Edris Gunn
Sports Editor. . . . . .Jerry. Reedy
Assistant. . . . . .Harold Hunt
Club Editor. . . . . Fred Ray Blocker
Assistant. . . . . .Lorraine Jackson
Photography Editor. . . . . .John Allen Henley
Campusology Editor. . . . . .Joyce Jenson
Assistant. . . . . .J. B. Parks
Snaps. . . . . Williston Chason

BUSINESS STAFF

Sue Bennett
   and .... Business Managers
Jean Hatcher

Clayton Young............. Assistant Business Manager

Katherine Cox..................... Circulating Editor

Frances Hammond .... Secretary

Dean John H. Banks................... Faculty Advisor

THE TOM TOM

"TOWARD A BIGGER AND BETTER E.C.J.C."

—STAFF—

EDITOR-IN-CHIEF.................Betty Lynn.Johnson
ASSOCIATE EDITOR......................Bobbie Gillis
BUSINESS MANAGER......................Paul Perry
EXCHANGE EDITOR........................Doris Poole
PRODUCTION MANAGER................Tom Chisolm
ASST. PRODUCTION MGR...............Marcella Webb
CIRCULATION MANAGER..............Kitty Moreland
ASSISTANTS TO CIRCULATION MANAGER—Mildred Nelson, Lillian Hardy, Ellen Boutwell

COLUMNISTS......Rosalie Burkes, Elaine Long, Delores Ball
SOCIAL EDITOR....................Myrtice McMullen
SPORTS EDITOR..........................Joe Bennett
CARTOONIST................................Jerry Reedy
REPORTERS—Gay Williams, Bernard Stamper, tommy Jean Hatcher, Marian Graham, Naomi McCraw, Betty McCraney
ADVERTISING STAFF—tommy Duke, Joyce Billings, Janice Hunt, Clayton Young, Lorraine Jackson, Margaret Shannon, L. H. Smith, Carl Williams.
TYPISTS—Margaret taylor, Doris Poole, Frances Warwick, • Grace Green, Ruth Mason, Juanita Lay.
SPONSOR...........................Miss Una Harris

Classes

The President's Message
To The Graduating Classes

This copy of the WO-HE-LO will become one of your prized possessions. You will realize this immediately upon receiving it, and it will grow more valuable with the years. In the future you will spend many hours poring over its pages. The snap shots, autographs, and "posed" pictures will bring back many tender associations. The peculiar styles of dress will amaze you. Your interest in friends will be rekindled.

The WO-HE-LO will be a tangible device for binding you together with your Alma Mater. It will refresh your memories of the days when we all worked, learned, and played together at East Central Junior College. There will be the memory of inspiring teachers, of friendly counselings, of challenging messages both public and private. There will be the memory of great music programs, interesting and stimulating assembly speakers, of exciting basketball games (remember Decatur 50—Goodman 48). There will be the memory of working together in the many student organizations and of participating in student "sessions." There will also be the memory of many quiet hours spent in study and reflection.

Finally, the WO-HE-LO, I hope, will be a stimulator of pleasant memories and a challenger to further growth. It will record some of the events, personalities, and scenes of the great period of your lives when you were growing up to understand a great deal more about the world and your own powers. It will remind you of the days when you really were developing the ability of your minds to think clearly without prejudice, when you were broadening your tastes and appreciation of the good and the beautiful; when you were developing your sense of responsibility for the powers given into your hands.

May this book and everything about this institution challenge you to useful living. This is our hope.

Your friend,
L. O. TODD

The Sophomore Class

Kenneth Hunter.........................President
Carl Williams.......................Vice-President
Ruth Mason...........................Secretary
Frances Hunt.........................Treasurer
Alene Martin..........................Reporter
Mrs. Stella Newsome ....Sponsor
J. H. Banks...........................Sponsor

27

Sophomores

SUE BENNETT .... Louisville
Business   May 2
  Pres. Wesley Foundation, Pres. IRC, V.-Pres.
  Y Council, Sec. and Treas. YWCA, Annual
  Staff, FTA, Vesper.
    "A perfect woman, nobly planned,
    To warn, to comfort, and command."
DIXIE BRIGGS .... Scooba
            Religious Education
  Wesley Foundation, IRC, Dramatic Club.
    "There's nothing ill can dwell in such a
    temple."
TOM CHISHOLM .... Philadelphia
  Wesley Foundation, Dramatic Club, IRC,
  Glee Club.
    "He is as full of valor as of kindness;
    princely in both."
WILDA COOK .... Decatur
            Liberal Arts
    "The hand that hath made you fair hath
    made you good."
JO COOPER .... Conehatta
  Commerce   July 20
  Reporter of Vesper, FTA, BSU, YWCA, Y
  Council, Dramatic Club.
    "Earth seems more sweet to live upon;
    More full of love because of her."

NONIE PEARL COWARD .... Ludlow
  Commerce .   November 5
  Vesper, Noon-Day, YWCA.
    "Build on and make thy castles high and
    fair."
KATHERINE COX .... Philadelphia
  Home Economics   December 17
    Dramatic Club, Vice-President Home Ec. Club,
    Reporter Wesley Foundation, President Morn-
    ing Watch, Noon-Day, Vesper, YWCA, Y
    Council, Annual Staff.
      "Be to her virtue very kind,
      Be to her faults a little blind."
GURVIS CUMBERLAND .... Philadelphia
            Teachers
  FTA, YMCA.
    "A good natured fellow, a trustworthy
    friend."
LAVERNE GIBBS .... Lake
  Teachers   May 5
  Glee Club, BSU, FTA, Vesper.
    "Gather ye rosebuds while ye may."
THELMA GOODIN .... Louisville
  Teachers   June 17
  Vice-President FTA, Dramatic Club, Glee Club,
  Morning Watch.
    "Her voice was ever soft, gentle and low,
    An excellent thing in woman."

ANNIE LEE GORDON .... Decatur
Commerce
Cheer-Leader.
"The eternal feminine draws her on."
WILMA RITH GORDON .... House
Teachers   July 19
FTA, Vesper.
"What wisdom can you find that is greater
than kindness."
DON GRAHAM .... Dixon
Agriculture   October 10
Reporter of Dramatic Club, Y Council, Wesley
Foundation, YWCA, Noon-Day.
"You are a king by your own fireside, as
as any monarch on his throne."
GRACE GREEN .... Walnut Grove
Teachers   February 4
President BSU, Morning Watch, Dramatic
Club, Noon-Day, Vesper, President FTA, Y
Council, YWCA.
"Do your duty and leave the rest to
heaven."
FRANCES HAMMOND .... Louisville
Liberal Arts   November 5
Dramatic Club, Glee Club, IRC, Wesley
Foundation, YWCA, Vesper, Noon-Day, Annual
Staff, Paper Statt.
"To know her is to love her."

TOMMYE JEAN HATCHER .... Calhoun
Teachers   July 1
Reporter Y Council, Vice-President YWCA,
Vesper, Wesley Foundation, IRC, Dramatic
Club, FTA, Morning Watch, Noon-Day, Annual
Staff, Paper Staff.
"Seeing only what is fair, sipping only
what is sweet."
NELL HERD .... Stratton
Liberal Arts   May 8
"Her soul is like a srat and dwells apart."
FRANCES HUNT .... Forest
Commerce   May 24
Noon-Day, Treas. of Vesper, Reporter of BSU,
Sec. Dramatic Club, Y Council, Morning
Watch, YWCA.
"A creature not too bright or good for
human nature's daily food."
HAROLD HUNT .... Newton
Business
"One foot in sea, and one on shore,
To one thing constant never."
JANICE HUNT .... Calhoun
Teachers   December 19
Glee Club, Dramatic Club, FTA, Morning
Watch, Noon-Day, YWCA, BSU, Paper Staff.
"I fling my soul on high with a new
endeavor."

Sophomores

Sophomores

KENNETH HUNTER .... Decatur
                Agriculture
  President Sophomore Class, Vice-President
  Youth Fellowship, Annual Staff.
    "He thinks like a philosopher and acts like
    a king."
ELTON HURT .... Louisville
  Lab. Tech.   May 20
  Y Council, YWCA, BSU, Vice-President BSU
  Noon-Day.
    "Her lovliness I never knew until she smiled
    on me."
BETTY IDON .... Morton
  Teachers   November 30
  President Home Ec. Club, FTA, Morning
  Watch, Dramatic Club.
    "A violet by a mossy stone,
    Half hidden from the eye."
LORRAINE JACKSON .... Decatur
  Liberal Arts   August 22
  Glee Club, Dramatic Club, Wesley Foundation,
  Paper Staff, Annual Staff, President IRC.
    "Your eyes blue depths are lifted,
    With love and friendship stirred."
JEAN GIBBON JOHNSON .... Newton
            Liberal Arts
    "Give me a spirit that on this life's rough sea,
    Loves to have its sails filled with
    a lusty wind."

ROBERT GAINES JORDON .... Decatur
            Lab. Tech.
    "Everyone knows him and appreciates
    him."
CATHERINE KEMP .... Meridian
  Teachers   March 9
  Sec. and Treas. of FTA; Home Ec Club, Vesper,
  Annual Staff, Dramatic Club.
    "Like a high-born maiden,
    In a palace tower."
MARY RUBY KEMP .... Louisville
  Teachers   September 20
  Dramatic Club, Reporter of FTA, Vesper,
  YWCA, BSU, Morning Watch.
    "The noblest mind, the best contentment
    has."
LAVERNE LEWIS .... Morton
  Teacher   September 19
  Home Ec. Club, FTA, Vesper, YWCA, Wesley
  Foundation, Noon-Day.
    "Exceeding fair she was."
ELAINE LONG .... Norton
  Teacher   December 28
  FTA, Vesper, BSU, YWCA, Noon-Day.
    "A mind at peace with all below,
    A heart whose love is innocent."

MILDRED LOVORN .... Calhoun
Teachers   November 17
  Sec. Glee Club, Chorister of Morning Watch,
  Y Council, YWCA, Dramatic Club, Wesley
  Foundation, Noon-Day, Annual Staff.
    "Pure is the spirit that dwells within and
    shines alike on all."
THEDRA LUKE .... Philadelphia
Liberal Arts   November 19
  Treas. of IRC, Vesper, YWCA, Y Council, Glee
  Club, Home Ec. Club, Noon-Day, Wesley Foun-
  dation.
    "Her eyes as stars of twilight fade,
    Like twilight too her dusky hair."
ELEANOR McCRANEY .... Decatur
Lab. Tech.   October 1
  Basketball, Dramatic Club, Glee Club.
    "She has proved herself loyal, courteous,
    and true."
CORALYN McHAHAN .... Union
          Teachers
    "Those who meet her are never
    disappointed,
    Those who know her never regret it."
FRED McMULLAN .... Stratton
          Auto Mechanics
    "Surely a man of truth and right,
    You'll recognize this just on sight."

MELTON McMULLAN .... Decatur
Social Studies   October 2
  Vice-President IRC, Paper Staff, Dramatic Club.
    "Not too serious, not too gay, But a rare
    good fellow when it comes to play."
MYRTICE McMULLAN .... Decatur
Liberal Arts   October 14
  Paper Staff.
    "A countenance in which did meet,
    Sweet record promises as sweet."
GAY NELL MAJURE .... Decatur
Liberal Arts   November 9
  Dramatic Club.
    "There is a garden in her face,
    Where roses and while lilies grow."
ALENE MARTIN .... Birmingham, Ala.
Liberal Arts   October 1
  President Wesley Foundation, Reporter of
  Sophomore Class, Y Council, Dramatic Club,
  Reporter of Glee Club, Annual Staff, IRC,
  YWCA, Vesper, Home-Ec. Club.
    "A sweet attractive kind of grace,
    A full assurance given by looks."
RUTH MASON .... Decatur
Liberal Arts   March 28
  Dramatic Club, Glee Club, Annual Staff, Sec.
  Sophomore Class, Paper Staff.
    "Her calm gentle sweetness sets her apart
    from all."

Sophomores

Sophomores

LENORD NELSON .... Lawrence
Agriculture   May 1
"I can cheerfully take it now,
Or with equal cheerfulness wait."
MARY PARKES .... Conehatta
          Lab. Tech.
Chorister of YWCA, Noon-Day and Vesper,
President of Y Council, President BSU, Morning
Watch, Glee Club, Annual Staff.
"Grace was in her steps, heaven in her eyes,
In every gesture dignity and love."
ETOILE PEAGLER .... Morton
Commerce   October 2
Vesper, BSU, YWCA, Noon-Day.
"Her very goodness shines over her like a
halo."
DORIS PEARSON .... Conehatta
Teacher   · August 15
Vesper, Noon-Day, FTA, YWCA.
"I strove with none for none was worth
my strife."
KATHERINE REEVES .... Decatur
Teachers   August 5
Glee Club, Basketball.
"I am merry when I hear sweet music."

ILLENE RICHIE .... Philadelphia
Teachers   May 1
Editor of Annual, Cheer Leader, President
Glee Club, Vice-President Dramatic Club, FTA,
Pianist for Noon-Day, Vesper, **BSU**, YWCA,
Y Council.
"Bright star. 'Would I as steadfast as thou
art.'"
HUGENE RIVERS .... Union
Commerce   November 18
Vesper, Noon-Day, Wesley Foundation,
YWCA.
"If to her share some female errors fall,
Look on her face and you will forget them
all."
EMOGENE SMITH .... Noxapater
          Commerce
YWCA, Vesper, BSU.
"Her air, her manners; all who saw admired;
Courteous, tho coy, and gentle tho retired."
L. H. SMITH .... Noxapater
Agriculture   April 28
BSU, Y Council, BTU, YMCA, Noon-Day, Paper
Staff.
"Every inch a gentleman."
FRED TALBERT .... Noxapater
          Science
"He preaches well that lives well."

LILLIAN TAYLOR .... Decatur
Home Economics
Wesley Foundation, IRC, Home Ec. Club.
"She is a portion of the loveliness which
she makes more lovely."

LOUISE VANCE .... Decatur
Liberal Arts
Noon-Day, Morning Watch, Vesper, Glee
Club, YWCA, Y Council, Wesley Foundation.
"The sweetest thing that ever grew
beside a human door."

FRANCES WARWICK .... Lena
Commerce   May 31
Glee Club, BSU.
"I live not in myself, but I become a
portion of that around me."

MARCELLE WEBB .... Ringold
Commerce   February 15
Sec. Vesper, YWCA, BSU.
"A wise player accepts his throws and
scores them."

SARA WEBB .... Noxapater
Lab. Tech.   November 28
Dramatic Club, Glee Club, Home Ec Club,
Sec. and Treas. of Wesley Foundation, Sec. of
Noon-Day, Treas. Y Council, President of
Vesper.
"A woman of sense and manners is the
most delicate part of God's creation."

MARY ELIZABETH WILKERSON .... Lake
Teachers
"Her ways are the ways of pleasantness,
and all her paths peace."

CARL WILLIAMS .... Little Rock
Agriculture   January 8
BSU, YMCA, Y Council, Paper Staff, Dramatic
Club, Noon-Day, Vice-President Sophomore
Class.
"A very perfect gentle knight."

CHARLES WILLIAMSON .... Little Rock
Agriculture   August 23
"Willingness accompanys his ability."

DEAN WILSON .... Stratton
Commerce   April 24
"Come in the evening or come in the
morning, Come when you're looked for
or come without warning."

PRINTICE STUART .... Philadelphia
Agriculture   September 29
YMCA.
"Self-reverence, self knowledge, self-con-
trol,
These three alone lead life to sovereign
power."

Sophomores

Sophomores

HUGH CHISHOLM . . . . Philadelphia.
Commerce   March 23
   "The greater the man, the greater the
   courtesy."

BONNIE HUDSON . . . . New Albany
Lab. Tech.   February 5
   Noon-Day, Morning Watch, Vesper, Glee
   Club, Dramatic, Wesley Foundation, YWCA.
   "She doeth little kindness which most leave
   undone or despise."

HILDA JO JOHNSON . . . . Harperville
Commerce   March 7
   Vice-President Morning Watch, Vesper,
   YWCA, Wesley Foundation, Y Council,
   Noon-Day.
   "Like a rose embowered in her own green
   leaves."

Freshman Day

Can you ever forget? Stringy hair and shiny noses! The smell of bitterweeds—dresses on backwards—books in suitcases. It would take a mother to love us. The day is over—tired, but hot, and a bit happy— Let me to a shower.

The Freshmen Class

OFFICERS

David Woodruff..........................President
John. Allen Henley ....Vice-President
Ruth Henry............................Secretary
J. B. Parks............................Treasurer
Joyce Jensen...........................Reporter
Clayton Young....................Sergeant-at-Arms
Betty Short............................Sponsor
Robert James ....Sponsor

Freshmen

Aubrey Adams .... Conehatta
Grady Adcock .... Union
Frances Aycock .... Hickory

Mildred Aycock .... Decatur
Delores Ball .... Louisville
Jo Bennett .... Louisville

Joyce Billings .... Jackson
Ellen Blackwell .... Montrose
Fred Ray Blocker .... Edinburg

Harold Boler .... Neshoba
Ellen Boutwell .... Newton
Rosalie Burkes .... Edinburg

Nancy Burnham .... Harperville
Charles Cannon .... McDonald
Williston Chasson ...... Port St. Jo, Florida

Thomas Chisolm .... Collinsville
Paul Chunn .... Philadelphia
Iris Clark .... Noxapater

Freshmen

Ruth Crane .... Lake
Eldon Davis .... Morton
Billy Dearman .... Newton

Maggie Sue Dorman .... Union
Tommie Helen Duke .... Newton
James Edwards .... Union

Maxine Estes .... Noxapater
Jonnie Freeman .... Decatur
Paul Fulton .... Louisville

Rachel Gainey .... Tuscola
Rilla Jean Gatewood .... Forest
Charlene Gay .... Lake

Bobbie Gillis .... Philadelphia
Rex Gordon .... Union
Clariece Graham .... Decatur

Edris Gunn .... Lena
Ivan Hand .... Collinsville
Lola Harbour .... Union

Freshmen

Lillian Hardy .... Union
Jo Hardwick .... Louisville
Sara Frances Harrison .... Hickory

Minnie Mae Hawkins .... Jackson
Hope Hawthorne .... Carthage
John Allen Henley .... Philadelphia

Ruth Henry .... Bradley
Marjorie Hobby .... Philadelphia
W. D. Holifield .... Laurel

Alton Harris .... Decatur
Joyce Harris Jensen .... Louisville
Betty Lynn Johnson .... Walnut Grove

Herman Johnson .... Philadelphia
Imogene Johnson .... Decatur
Doris Jones .... Bay Springs

Juanita Lay .... Lena
Rebecca Lofton .... Philadelphia
Hugh McCraney .... Decatur

Freshmen

Naomi McCraw . . . . Harperville
Bessie McDonald . . . . Lena
Ray McGee . . . . Center

Gwendolyn May . . . . Decatur
Ben Minshew . . . . Dosville
Mildred Nelson . . . . Union

Sybil Pace . . . . Conehatta
J. B. Parks . . . . Lawrence
Paul Perry . . . . Decatur

Lynn Phillips . . . . Newton
Doris Poole . . . . Collinsville
Buford Posey . . . . Philadelphia

Madell Price . . . . Noxapater
Carolyn Rea . . . . Philadelphia
Elouise Rea . . . . Philadelphia

Fleteher Redd Jr . . . . Union
Dale Reynolds . . . . Neshoba
Beverly Ricks . . . . Union

Freshmen

Johnnie Roberts .... Louisville
J. B. Round .... Newton
Louise Russel .... Union

Etoile Sessums .... Forest
Margaret Shannon .... Decatur
Annie Lou Shumaker .... McCool

Georgia Nell Simms .... Bay Springs
Estell Sistrunk .... Walnut Grove
Bryce Sloan .... Louisville

Howard Smith .... Union
Marlene Smith .... Union
Daphne Snellgrove .... New Orleans, La.

Katherine Stuart .... Louisville
Margaret Taylor .... Union
R. G. Taylor .... Laurel

Rebecca Taylor .... Philadelphia
Samuel Taylor .... Edinburg
Nelda Thrash .... Conehatta

Freshmen

Rodney Thomas .... Madder
Emogene Trusdale .... Ofahoma
Carl Underwood .... Sebastopoc

Margaret Vence .... Decatu
Dorlos Jean Vaughn .... Houstor
Molly Wade .... Louisville

Jewel Waltman .... Lake
Joyce Ruth Watkins .... Lena
Floyce Dean Whinery .... Edinburg

Ruth Wiggs .... Decatu
Dale Wilkerson .... Fores
Glynn Wilkerson .... Lake

Lawrence Williams .... Little Rocl
Gay Williams .... Dossvill
Elizabeth Willis .... Noxapate

David Woodruff .... Louisvill
Glenn Womack .... Mante
Clayton Young .... Neshob

Freshmen

Shed Young .... Mathiston
Kitty Moreland .... Lena
Thomas Monore Mizango .... Decatur

TIMES

WORTH

RECORDING

Follow me. I'll show you what's happening here at school—inside and out. It's rather queer 'cause every year when the first signs of spring appear, I start to prowling, and since this is my first year in college I find many key holes to peep through to gain information.

Gosh, what's this! Something that comes through "Hodge Podges" key hole is burning my nose and making the tears flow like wine. My! my! Mr. Paskins don't tell me that some one has tried to gas you . . . Or is this just a mutual agreement between you and Ritchie. Maybe Mr.. Banks can tell us all about it.

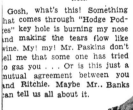

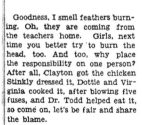

The only way to get into the girls dormitory is to go after the Coca Cola bottles, so grab an empty and let's go. Look at the ole arbor vita shaking—Um—Oh pardon me, Ivan. I didn't know you and Edris were behind it.

.Not so fair a damsel do I know than that gal who is editor of this paper, but all the boys say she has ideas all her own and most of them concern journalism.

Campus Key Hole

Goodness, I smell feathers burning. Oh, they are coming from the teachers home. Girls, next time you better try to burn the head, too. And too, why place the responsibility on one person? After all, Clayton got the chicken Stinkly dressed it, Dottie and Virginia cooked it, after blowing five fuses, and Dr. Todd helped eat it, so come on, let's be fair and share the blame.

Tommie Jean, how was the picnic the other Sunday. Rebecca said it was OK. Too bad you couldn't call Joyce's mother from Linwood.

45

THE HIGH SCHOOL
CLASS OFFICERS

SENIORS

President........................Edwin Miller
Vice-President..................James Edwards
Secretary....................Benoline Meador
Treasurer........................ R. D. Kelly
Reporter........................Nell Pearson
Sponsor.................. Mrs. Janie Sullivan

JUNIORS

President....................Danny Shannon
Vice-President..............Benard Stamper
Secretary................Laverne Pennington
Treasurer................... Malcolm Jones
Reporter....................Marian Graham
Sponsor.................. Virgiana Clements

Seniors

Annie Merle Addy
  Jane Brand
    George Ellis Crawford Jr.

Raymond Golden
  Beatrice Harris
    Maxwell Herrington

Edna Earl Hillman
  Dorothy Jordon
    Laverne Van Etten

June Hollingworth
  Margie McElhenney
    Louis McMullan

Sidney McNeil
  Annie Lou Massey
    Benoline Meador

Edna Meltz
  Edwin Miller
    Eugenia Moore

Seniors

Nell Pearson
Sammye Massey
Clara Mae Ricks

Grover Shumaker
Sara Joy Smith
Issac Valentine

Mary Helen Valentine
Walter Williams
Otis Hardy

Juniors

Frances Addy
John "Tootsie" Blount
Norma Lee Brand

William "Corky" Capps
Lyn Densom
Mariam Graham

Malcolm Jones
Lottie Frank McElhenney
Betty McCraney

Juniors

Otto Malone
  Laverne Pennington
    Carolyn Perry

Jean Quattlebaum
  Calvin Roberts
    Jerry Reedy

R. G. Smith
  Benard Stamper
    Evelyn Rowezee

Danny Shannon
  Billie J. "Snorter" Thames
    David Hopkins

Annelle Thornton
  Harold Pennington

20263

49

Some go to class.

Some go crazy.

Some love to play.

Some stay in.

Have it

Some live to love.

Some go out.

Some go in crowds.

Some go alone.

Your Way

Some live to eat.

Some love to live.

Some eat to live.

Don Graham

Mr E. C. J. C.

Miss E. C. J. C.

Illene Richie

Lorraine Jackson

The May Queen

and her Court

Lillian Taylor, Katherine Cox, Mildred Aycock, Marlene Smith, Gay Williams, Ruby May Milner, and Gay Nell Majure.

MAY DAY 1945

Frances Hammond

Betty Idom

THE B

Joyce Billings

Edris Gunn

UTIES

Sara Frances Harrison

Janie Hawkins

Mildred Lovorn

Williston Chasen

THE FA

John Allan Henley

Joyce Jenson

ORITES

Louise Vance

Billy Dearman

Most Charming Girl
Ruth Henry

Most Versatile Boy
Kenneth Hunter

Most Handsome Boy
Carl Williams

Most Versatile Girl
Sue Bennett

Who's

Who

Most Talented Girl
Sarah Webb

Wittiest Girl
Friendliest Girl
Joyce Jensen

Wittiest Boy
Harold Hunt

Most Talented Boy
Typical Freshman Boy
Fred Ray Blocker

Typical Freshman Girl
Molly Wade

Friendliest Boy
Best Dressed Boy
John A. Henley

Cutest Girl
Rebecca Taylor

Best Dressed Girl
Katherine Kemp

Cutest Boy
Billy Dearman

At E. C. J. C.

Most Intellectual Girl
Betty Lynn Johnson

Best Boy Athlete
David Woodruff

Most Intellectual Boy
Melton McMullun

Best Girl Athlete
Marcelle Webb

63

Who's Who
At
High School

Mr. Decatur High
Dolan Coghlan

Miss Decatur High
Benoline Meadows

Most Handsome Boy
James Edwards

Best Boy Athlete
Max Herrington

Most Beautiful Girl
Margurite Graham

Billy Jackson Thames

Mary Helen Valentine

Malcolm Jones

Campus Favorites

Dorthy Buntyn

William "Corky" Capps

Evelyn Rowzee

Most Intellectual Girl	Most Intellectual Boy	Most Talented Girl	Most Talented Boy
June Hollingsworth	Sidney McNeil	Sammye Massey	Jerry Reedy

Campus

Best Dressed Girl
Jane Brand

Girl Most Likely to Succeed   Boy Most Likely to Succe
Marian Graham   Bernard Stamper

Best Dressed Boy
Shed Young

Most Versatile Girl
Laverne Pennington

Cutest Girl
Nell Pearson

Cutest Boy
Danny Shannon

Most Versatile Boy
R. J. Smith

Favorites

Most Charming Girl
Carolyn Perry

Most Polite Boy
Raymond Golden

Friendliest Girl
Frances Addy

Friendliest Boy
John Blount

Grandmother, how's
the baby?

Waiting for "chow."

Teased?

Oh you veteran.

Trig is impossible
Chemistry is as bad:

Lit's all in a fog,
But these times re-
main—

Caught!

March hares!

Toothache or heart-
ache?

Don't tell Bessie.   Handsome?   Why Billie.

Clear in our memories

As the years come
and go.

All the ladies' man.   The Bookworm.

Every campus has one.

A gentleman's agree-   Polishing the apple.   Here we are boys.
ment.

Around the Campus

1. The Reverend
2. Just snooping
3. Etcetera
4. Where old friends meet.
5. Sounds interesting
6. At ease
7. A joke
8. The latest edition
9. The return of the "Bluebird"
10. The reason for the new rules
11. Going home

Organizations

Sue Bennett, Jo Cooper, Bobbie Gillis, Edris Gunn, John Allan Henley, Joyce Jenson, Doris Jones, Bessie McDonald, Kitty Mooreland, Ruth Crane, Nancy Burnham, Fred Ray Blocker, Etoile Sessums, Georgia Nell Sims, Clayton Young, Hilda Jo Johnson, Carl Williams, Louise Vance, L. H. Smith, Illene Richie, Mary Parkes, Alene Martin, Thedra Luke, Mildred Lovorn, Mary Ruby Kemp, Marlene Smith, Frances Warwick, Molly Wade, Lillian Taylor, Tom Chisolm, Elton Hurt, Frances Hunt, Jean Hatcher, Don Graham, Grace Green, Katherine Cox, Willie Chasen.

The "Y" Council

BOBBIE GILLIS .... President
GRACE GREEN .... Vice-President
MARY RUBY KEMP .... Secretary
SARAH WEBB .... Treasurer
JEAN HATCHER .... Reporter

The "Y" Council is composed of all the officers of the various religious organizations on the campus. It meets each Monday night to plan the various religious activities to be carried on the campus.

Y. M. and Y. W. C. A.

OFFICERS

CLAYTON YOUNG .... President
JEAN HATCHER .... Vice-President
JOHN ALLAN HENLEY .... Vice-President
MARLENE SMITH .... Secretary-Treasurer
ILLENE RICHIE .... Pianist
MILDRED LOVORN .... Chorister
MRS. SULLIVAN .... Sponsor

PURPOSE

Y.M. and Y.W.C.A. meet weekly and the purpose of this organization is to develop Christian fellowship among the boys and girls on the campus and to make more Christian leaders.

B S U

OFFICERS

GRACE GREEN .... President

NANCY BURNHAM .... First Vice-President

CLAYTON YOUNG .... Second Vice-President

RUTH CRANE .... Third Vice-President

GEORGIE NELL SIMS .... Secretary

BESSIE McDONALD .... Chorister

ILLENE RICHIE .... Pianist

FRANCES HUNT .... Reporter

THE REV. HOGAN .... Advisor

PURPOSE

The B.S.U. is a connecting link between the college and the local church in the college center. It is not an organization but organized program for all Baptist students and students of Baptist preference on the campus. It is maintained by the B.S.U. Council, which is elected annually by a nominating committee taken from the B.S.U. as a whole. The B.S.U. meets weekly in the auditorium of the Baptist Church. Rev. W. A. Hogan is sponsor and Mrs. Janie Sullivan is the faculty advisor.

Wesley Foundation

OFFICERS

ALENE MARTIN .... President

WILLISTON CHASON .... Vice-President

SARAH WEBB .... Secretary and Treasurer

KATHERINE COX .... Reporter

PURPOSE

The Wesley Foundation is a campus organization made up of those students whose interests and affiliation are in accord with the Methodist Church. It promotes good fellowship and religious fervor and provides inspirational atmosphere for its members. It also acts as a connecting link between the student campus life and the work of the Youth Fellowship in the church. The Foundation meets each Thursday evening in the home of its sponsor, Mrs. W. W. Newsome.

Girls Vesper

OFFICERS

SARAH WEBB .... President
BOBBIE GILLIS .... First Vice-President
THEDRA LUKE .... Second Vice-President
FRANCES HUNT .... Treasurer
MARCELLE WEBB .... Secretary
MOLLY WADE .... Reporter
DORIS JONES .... Chorister
ILLENE RICHIE .... Pianist
MRS. JACKSON .... Sponsor

In order to deepen the spiritual life of the dormitory girls, it has been the custom for many years to have a short devotional service twice each week in the dormitory lobby. These short services give the school day the right ending.

Noonday Prayer Service

OFFICERS

FRED RAY BLOCKER .... President
LOUISE VANCE .... Vice-President
SARAH WEBB .... Treasurer
MILDRED LOVORN .... Chorister
ILLENE RICHIE .... Pianist

Morning Watch

OFFICERS

Katherine Cox...........................President
Jo Johnson...........................Vice-President
Mildred Lovorn........................Chorister
Bessie McDonald ....Pianist
Etoile Sessums...........................Reporter

College International Relations Club

MEMBERS

Aubery Adams, De Lores Ball, Sue Bennett, Joe Bennett, Joyce Billings, Ellen Blackwell, Fred Ray Blocker, Dixie Briggs, Nancy Burnham, Charles Cannon, Williston Chason, Windford Eason, Johnny Freeman, Paul Fulton, Bobbie Gillis, Rex Gordon, Clariece Graham, Don Graham, Frances Hammond, tommye Jean Hatcher, John Allen Henley, Ruth Henry, Lorraine Jackson, Herman Johnson, Alene Martin, Thomas Mazingo, Naomi McCraw, Melton McMullan, Kitty Moreland, Leonard Nelson, Elaine Long, Thedra Luke, Buford Posey, Lynn Phillips, Dale Reynolds, Beverly Ricks, Margaret Shannon, Lillian taylor, Rebecca taylor, Charles Tingle, Molly Wade, Glenn Womack, Glen Wilkerson, Gay Williams, Clayton Young.

OFFICERS

SUE BENNETT	President	LORRAINE JACKSON
MELTON McMULLAN	V.-President,	CLAYTON YOUNG
BOBBIE GILLIS	Secretary	BOBBIE GILLIS
THEDRA LUKE	Treasurer	THEDRA LUKE
LORRAINE JACKSON	Reporter	RUTH HENRY
	Sponsor	C. W. PASKINS

Newton County Agricultural High School
I. R. C.

Purpose as stated in the Preamble of the I.R.C. Constitution:

"We the members of the International Relations Club do hereby affiliate ourselves for the sole purpose of free and informal discussion without reserve of international problems that affect us as individuals and as citizens of this country and the world so as to understand and lay a basic foundation in youth for the development and betterment of relations of all people of the world.'

I.R.C. has increased from four members to forty-five. The four members worked out the constitution as the project for the summer term of 1945.

A number of outstanding projects have been carried out: Organization of High School I.R.C. under the leadership of Vice-President Clayton Young. . . the Sadie Hawkins' celebration on November 3—Pan American Ball on April 20.

OFFICERS

President .... JUNE HOLLINGSWORTH
Vice-President .... SIDNEY McNEIL
Secretary .... EDWIN MILLER
Treasurer .... BENOLINE MEADOW
Reporter .... CAROLYN PERRY
Sponsor .... MISS CLEMENTS

MEMBERS

Frances Addy, Norma Lee Brand, Dot Buntyn, William Capps, Raymond Golden, June Hollingsworth, Laverne Idon, Otto Malone, Betty McCraney, Richard McMullan, Sidney McNeil, Benoline Meador, Edna Meltz, Edwin Miller, Eugenia Moore, Laverne Pennigton, Carolyn Perry, Jean Quattlebaun, Jerry Reedy, Evelyn Rowzee, Walter Williams.

The Home Economics Club

MEMBERS

Catherine Kempt, Laverne Lewis, Thedra Luke, Sara Webb, Mary Parkes, Nancy Burnham, Alene Martin, Gay Williams, Emma Jean truesdale, Lynn Phillips, Georgia Nell Sims, Ruth Henry, Iris Clark, De Lores Ball, Naomi McCraw, Edris Gunn, Lillian taylor.

OFFICERS

BETTY IDOM .... President
KATHERINE COX .... Vice-President
MOLLY WADE .... Secretary and Treasurer
MISS RUTH BLANSHARD .... Sponsor

PURPOSE

The main purpose of the organization is to form a connecting link between the department and the home, to learn to use the tools and techniques of the profession, to gain poise and assurance in a variety of social situations, and to gain experience in legitimate means of raising money for the club.

MOTTO: "Today we follow; tomorrow we lead."

The Glee Club

MEMBERS

Laverne Gibbs, thelma Goodin, Frances Hammond, Benny Hudson, Fanice Hunt, Lorraine Jackson, Thedra Luke, Alene Martin, Mary Parks, Louise Vance, Frances Warick, Sarah Webb, Kitty Moreland, Gwendolyn May, Imogene Johnson, Joyce H. Jensen, Ruth Henry, Ruth Crane, Williston Chason. Nancy Burnham, De Lores Ball, Frances Aycock, Grady Aycock, R. G. taylor, Margaret taylor, Melba Jean Smith, Marlene Smith, Eloise Rea, Doris Poole, Lynn Phillips, Mildred Nelson, Junior Redd, Otto Malone, Don Graham, Douglas Caffey.

OFFICERS

Director .... MRS. CARRIE LEE MADDEN
President .... ILLENE RICHIE
Vice-President .... FRED R. BLOCKER
Secretary .... MILDRED LOVORN
Accompanist .... MARIAN GRAHAM

The Delta Psi Omega

FRED BLOCKER . . . . Cast Director
DON GRAHAM . . . . Stage Manager
JEAN HATCHER . . . . Vice Director
FRANCES HUNT . . . . Secretary

PLEDGES

Katherine Cox, Bobby Gillis, Edris Gunn, Bonny Hudson, Lorraine Jackson, Mary Ruby Kemp, Mildred Lovorn, Kitty Moreland, Illene Richie, Alene Martin, Sara Webb, Frances Hammond, Joyce Jensen, Betty Idom, Clayton Young.

PURPOSE

The Delta Psi Omega is the Junior College Honorary Dramatic Fraternity. Its purpose is to stimulate interest in the dramatic activities in E.C.J.C., to secure for the college all the advantages of a large national honorary fraternity, and to serve as a reward for dramatic efforts.

The Theatre Guild

OFFICERS

JOYCE JENSEN . . . . President
ILLENE RICHIE . . . . Vice-President
REBECCA LOFTON . . . . Secretary
DON GRAHAM . . . . Treasurer
FRANCES HUNT . . . . Reporter

The Future Teachers of America Club

Sue Bennett, Fred Ray Blocker, Rosalie Burkes, Ruth Crane, Jo Cooper, Gurvis Cumberland, Maxine Estes, Rilla Jean Gatewood, Charlene Gay, LaVerne Gibbs, Thelma Goodin, Wilma Ruth Gordon, Grace Green, Effie Haggard, Tommye Jean Hatcher, Janice Hunt, Betty Idom, Catherine Kemp, Mary Ruby Kemp, Laverne Lewis, Earlene Long, Elaine Long, Mildred Lovorn, Corolyn McMahen, Melton McMullan, Mildred Nelson, Doris Pearson, Lynn Phillips, Madell Price, Ilene Richie, Etoile Sessums, Joyce Ruth Watkins, Mary Elizabeth Wilkerson, Gay Williams, Floyce Dean Whinery, Ellen Blackwell.

OFFICERS

President .... GRACE GREEN
Vice-President .... THELMA GOODIN
Secretary .... JANICE HUNT
Reporter .... MARY RUBY KEMP

The purpose of the Future Teachers of America are: To acquaint teachers in train-ing with the history, ethics, and program of the organized teaching profession; to interest the best young men and women in education as a lifelong career; to encourage careful selection of persons admitted to schools which prepare teachers with emphasis on both character and scholarship; to seek thru the dissemination of information and thru higher standards of preparation to bring teacher supply and demand into a reason-able balance.

The Girl Reserves

Annie Merle Addy, Jane Brand, Dorothy Buntyn, Edna Earl Hillman, Dorothy Jordan, Annie Lou Massey, Edna Meltz, Eugenia Moore, Mary Anne Oliver, Carolyn Perry, Jean Quottlebaum, Evelyn Rowzee, Jessie Sims, tressie Sims, Mary Helen Valentine, Laverne Van Etten, Mary Sula Wansley.

CABINET

President	BENOLINE MEADOW
Vice-President	LAVERNE PENNINGTON
Secretary	SAMMYE MASSEY
Treasurer	NORMA LEE BRAND
Program Chairman	JUNE HOLLINGSWORTH
Service Chairman	SARAH JOY SMITH
Music Chairman	MARIAN GRAHAM
Social Chairman	FRANCES ADDY
Membership Chairman	MARY FRANCES SCHOCKLEY
Publicity Chairman	NELL PEARSON
Finance Chairman	MARGUERITE GRAHAM

Sponsor .... VIRGINIA CLEMENTS

G racious in manner
I mpartial in judgment
R eady for service
L oyal to friends

R eaching toward the best
E arnest in purpose
S eeing the beautiful
E ager for knowledge
R everent to God
V ictorious over self
E ver dependable
S incere at all times

Hi Y Club

CABINET MEMBERS

President .... GEORGE JAMES
Vice-President .... SHED D. YOUNG
Secretary and Treasurer ...... GLEN WOMACK
Reporter .... SIDNEY McNEIL

The Senior Hi-Y was organized in September 1945 and at the present there are 23 members. Recently, we have received our charter which affiliates us with the state and national organizations. Our programs are varied to meet the needs of present day boys. Occasionally we ask a speaker to visit our club and give a message to the boys. Other programs include Bible drill, moral subjects as Smut, Alcoholic Beverages, Profanity, Sportsmanship, and Boy-Girl relationship.

Home From The Wars

Herman Johnson, Alton C. Harris, James R. Jordon, John Prentice Stuart, Laverne Idom, Glenwood T. Womack, James R. Round, Samuel F. taylor, Lavell·L. Culpepper, Grover Shumaker, Charles E. Swain, James Steinwinder, Millie Mumm, Otto Malone, Bracy B. Graham, John C. Freeman, Willie H. McCraney, Johnnie B. Roberts, James Walter Edwards Jr., Kenneth T. Horne, Robert Robertson, Milton McMullan, Billy Blount, Windford. Eason, Leslie Carl Williams, Nolan F. Skinner, Maxwell G. Herrington, Grady Afcock, Henry Young, Benton Rex Gordon, David Hugh Chisholm, Louis H. Smith, R. G. taylor, B. P. Jackson Jr., J. C. McCann, William J. Ryals, Shed D. Young, Dallas W. Mathews, Burly D. Register, Robert Hillman Jr., James Rodney thomas, thomas M. Mazingo, Lewis Bailey, Raymond Golden, Leonard O. Nelson, Calvin Roberts Jr., William Osler Chapman, David Hopkins, Dewitt, Webster, Buford W. Posey, Herman Vaughn, Oscar G. Wilkerson, thomas A. Williams, Otis B. Hardy, Elmo M. Winstead, Carl M. Underwood, Franklin C. Rigney, James R. Walpole. Hermon L. Morris, Charles Tingle.

Athletics

The Football Squad

J. B. Parks, Billy Dearman, Malcolm Jones (All-State), Paul Fulton, Junior Crawford, Danny Shannon, Sidney McNeil, B. J. "Snorter" thames, Mitchell Warren, Eldon Davis, Joe Bennett, Max Herrington (All State), Kenneth Hunter, Don Graham, Jesse Huey, Jerry Reedy (Manager).

Illene Richie
Willie Chason
Joyce Jensen
Margaret
    Shannon

Annie Lee
    Gordon
"Corky" Capp
Kitty Moreland

The Girls Basketball Team

Coach Betty Short, Louise Russel, Melba Jean Smith, Katherine Reeves, Imogene Johnson, Dale Wilkerson, Imogene Smith, Eloise Rea, Marjorie Hobby, Marcelle Webb, Joyce Everette, Frances Aycock, Katherine Stewart, Joyce Jensen, Manager, Marlene Smith.

The E. C. J. C. Basketball Squad

The Warriors of East Central Junior College enjoyed a highly successful season this year, beating every team they played although some of these teams beat us in return engagements.

The Warriors were eliminated in the semi-finals of the State Tournament. They did succeed however in placing Fred McMullan on first string All State again. O. Q. Smith and Nolan Skinner made second string All State while Quinton Copeland made honorable mention.

THE SQUAD

Fred McMullan, Nolan Skinner, O. Q. Smith, Quinton Copeland, Charles Cannon, Monroe Mazzingo, Hugh McCraney, Dale Reynolds, Carl Underwood, Alton Harris, Johnny Freeman, Aubry Adams, Junior Hillman, Jo Bennett, Manager.

Joe Graham
Clell Hall
Lewis McMullan
Lavon Majure
Frank Meador
Corelton Graham
Donald Pennington
Curtis Monroe
Ellis Crawford
Edwin Miller
Mickey Pennington
Danny Shannon
Norman Thomas
R. D. Kelley
"Snorter" Thames
Paul Rigler
Gilbert Gilmore
Coach, Burley McCraw

High School Basketball Squads

Benoline Meador
Mary F. Shockley
Francis Addy
Thedra Johnson
Mary H. Valentine
Beatrice Harris
Bobby N. Hall
Neil Pearson
Mary Bailey
Maggie Ledlow
Laverne Van Etten
Janette Massey
Dorthy Gilmore
June Hollingsworth
Sammye Massey
Betty Short—Coach

The Boys

are Back

Campusology

One Moment Please

The remainder of this book is devoted to our staunch friends, OUR ADVERTISERS, without whose financial aid this book could not have been published. We leave you with the firm conviction that the remainder of this book will provide you with pleasant reminiscences just as surely as that which has gone before. The reading of these ads is sure to call back to your memory many true friendships which you made while in college, and cause you to live again many pleasant experiences. The staff of the WO-HE-LO wishes to say to our advertisers—

Our Sincere Thanks

CONGRATULATIONS

TO A

GOOD SCHOOL

IN A

GOOD PART

OF THE STATE

HENDERSON-MOLPUS

LUMBER COMPANY

THE COLE BROTHERS COMPANY

Wholesale Grocers

COLD STORAGE AND COFFEE ROASTERS

Philadelphia   Mississippi

E. S. Cole   W. F. Cole

W, D. Cole   M. A. Cole

WE SALUTE AND CONGRATULATE YOU

WO-HE-LO

On This, Your First Post-War Appearance, May You Live Long and Serve Well.

WE ARE THE ORIGINAL SPONSORS OF EAST CENTRAL JUNIOR COLLEGE

AND REJOICE IN YOUR SUCCESSES.

THE NEWTON RECORD

Serving Newton County and Area for 44 Years

Newton, Miss.

PEOPLES BANK OF UNION

Union and Decatur, Mississippi

BUCKLEY BROTHERS

WHOLESALE GROCERIES

Newton, Mississippi

HARDIN'S BAKERIES

A MISSISSIPPI INSTITUTION

Est. 1900

Meridian	Jackson
Tupelo	Columbus

BUY IT FOR FLAVOR . . .

A. DEWEESE LUMBER CO., INC.

Manufacturers of

YELLOW PINE LUMBER

Philadelphia   Mississippi

GARDNER'S FLORIST

Union, Mississippi

PHONE 2211

HOME OF FLOWERS FOR ALL OCCASIONS

Member of Florist's Telegraph Delivery Association

Compliments of

R. M. HENDRICK GRADUATE SUPPLY HOUSE

RINGS, INVITATIONS, DIPLOMAS

CAPS AND GOWNS

Jackson   Mississippi

MARS BROTHERS

GENERAL MERCHANTS AND COTTON BUYERS

WHOLESALE AND RETAIL

Philadelphia   Mississippi

SAVELL HATCHERY

GROCERY — MARKET — SEED

FULL-O-PEP FEED

SWIFT FERTILIZER

V. W. (Doc) Savell

Philadelphia   Mississippi

Lightning Source UK Ltd.
Milton Keynes UK
UKHW020025181218
334174UK00013B/2011/P

9 780331 384482